In the Tilling

poems by

Donna Isaac

Finishing Line Press
Georgetown, Kentucky

In the Tilling

Copyright © 2025 by Donna Isaac
ISBN 979-8-88838-912-6 First Edition
All rights reserved under International and Pan-American Copyright Conventions. No part of this book may be reproduced in any manner whatsoever without written permission from the publisher, except in the case of brief quotations embodied in critical articles and reviews.

Publisher: Leah Huete de Maines
Editor: Christen Kincaid
Cover Art: Donna Isaac, *Primitive: Sustenance* (watercolor)
Author Photo: Donna Isaac
Cover Design: Elizabeth Maines McCleavy

Order online: www.finishinglinepress.com
also available on amazon.com

Author inquiries and mail orders:
Finishing Line Press
PO Box 1626
Georgetown, Kentucky 40324
USA

Contents

In the Tilling

Shenandoah 1
The Tiptons 2
We Fill Up Our Days 3
Birthday Cake 4
The Thing About the Eye 5
Artichokes 6
Callinectes Sapidus 7
Kids 8
Carmen 9
Foreign Language 10
Berry is My Madeleine 11
College Freshmen/Mountains 13
Picking Asparagus 14
Meadows of Dan, Virginia 15

Where the River Ran 17
Grandmothers North and South 18
Avocados/Father 20
Apples/Father 22
Apricots 24
Mist 26
Off 27
Gardening 29
Worry, Worry, Worry 30
The Waczieleski Girls 31
Salmon 32
Reasons to Survive October 33
Distant Lightning 34
Circle Dance 36

On Blindness 40
The Art of Hearing 41
Teeth 43
Falling Down 44

What's Been Taken Away... 46
Italy, Late December.. 48
After Reading Bukowski... 49
Change of Heart.. 50
To Prepare and Care... 51
Till Death Do Us Part 52
On the Groaning Board.. 54
Early October, 2020.. 55
Omnivore... 58
Ode to Okra... 59
Mushrooms 61
Taste.. 62
Gluttony... 63
A Story of Yams 64
Taco King, Minnesota State Fair... 65
Tomatoes.. 66
Church Ladies... 67
On the Way to the Post Office... 68
End of November, 2020 69
Letting Go.. 70
Whither.. 71
Directions.. 72
Is this the zombie apocalypse
everyone is talking about?... 73
A Spring Trip After Russia
 Declares War 74
The Cheese Stands Alone 76
Task at Hand.. 77
May Day... 78

Notes and Acknowledgments

Preface

In the Tilling was sparked by my Hamline University MFA thesis, *Sustenance*, 2007 (Outstanding Poetry Thesis Award winner), which includes research on food writing, e.g., works by Ovid, Jean Anthelme Brillat-Savarin, and M.F.K. Fischer as well as others who, like me, are inspired by the gifts of the earth and sea and the joys of cooking; original poems often related to food; and collected recipes. In my formative years, my Virginia grandmother baked biscuits, Thanksgiving pies, and country hams; canned homemade ketchup, peaches, and pickles; made do with what little the family had like stewing tomatoes extended with scraps of bread. My Minnesota grandmother dabbled with Polish foods, apple pies, and spaghetti and meatballs, a recipe she inherited from her neighbor in St. Paul, Rose Totino of Totino Pizza fame. My Minnesota-born mother cooked almost every meal at home, learning along the way, and embracing Southern foodways since she had married a Virginian. I tripped along at these cooks' heels and enjoyed the work of the kitchen, the taste of food lovingly prepared. The book title comes from a poem that begins the collection, celebrating my family's penchant for gardening, particularly in Appalachian regions where I was raised; it is also a nod to my continuing to write poetry "late unto evening" as an older person living in the new millennium.

In the Tilling

The ancestors killed for food:
hogs shot, strung up, gutted; chickens axed, rabbits trapped.
      The ancestors turned ground, clods of red clay,
sowed seed beds, cucumber hills.
      The ancestors canned peaches, strung leather britches,
made ketchup, chow-chow, piccalilli, green tomato pie.
      They milked cows, smoked ham, churned butter.

      Like Antaeus, their strength came from earth.

This is the stuff of country music, porch swappin', the *Georgics*.

Crosshatches in my hands are dirty from working this morning
the soil of my garden. No amount of pumice
or progress removes the longitude within my palm.

      No amount of rainfall can wash these roots away.

A song goes up to the mountaintop,
      the one that resurrects those who remember the shed,
      the table of pies, the hand on the hoe.
Ghosts rise from tomato jars hot out of the bath,
in first green shoots, in muddy boots by the door.

The soul can be fertile like loam
      in the tilling, late, even unto evening.

Shenandoah

Child of the mountain, bare feet treading moss
dusty paths, you listen for your mother's voice
calling suppertime across the pinetops, pintos with ham,
warm rolls, and the juiciest peach slump of summer.
In the morning, strong coffee in a rosebloom cup,
grandmother feeding you wisdom from a mismatched spoon.
Out again into the hills for cold creek wading,
copperhead awareness among rocks, rhododendron.
Under a blue dome your sister dances beneath a willow,
wind moving green-lit branches.
Fetterless and fearless, friends on a tire swing
propel out over a brown river, hollers ringing the oxbow,
burnished boy rising out of ripples 'round your heart.
Long shadows chill sunny girls atop a palisade,
bunching rumpled coverlets to take home, to pin on a line.
Dusk fingers evening frets, fireflies wink,
flickers of love beneath a starlit sky.

The Tiptons

They were our neighbors in Tennessee,
down the street, a passel of boys and one girl
named Anita, half-Cherokee, all cheekbones
and long limbs. Anita owned a bucking horse,
Fury, who reared up on my brother and ran
me into barbed wire, the scar still on my calf.
Their daddy made sipping 'shine and gave it
to the menfolk in Mason jars.
All us kids had picnics in summer,
spitting watermelon seeds in the grass.
My sister saw Billy T. naked, peeling off his bathing
suit near the back creek, sacred sight.
The four boys were wild, our hearts' desire.
They bow-hunted in the mountains,
strung up deer bled-out beneath a tree.
They ate squirrel stew in grayish gravy.
Once Anita and I rode horses on Roan Mountain,
purple rosebay all around. Fury and Anita
took the lead, her rope slinging side-to-side
as we trotted down a dappled path,
red-tailed hawk rising like a song.

We Fill Up Our Days

The snow is white and creamy
like porch milk in a glass bottle
when I was a girl who sat on a metal box
that held the empties. *Clink, clink*
in a carrier heralded the milkman's
early delivery, rain, snow, or not.
I wouldn't mind the milkman coming 'round
as in my girlhood, friendly sorts, these delivery
men—even an eggman who brought eggs
slightly warm from the nest. My mother
gave this farmer one of our Easter chicks
turned pecking rooster that had to be confined
to a clawfoot tub. I remember a boy
who tucked the newspaper inside screen doors
to prevent wetness who collected every Saturday,
going house-to-house, getting an extra quarter
or four for a job well done. In summer, the ice-cream man
passed by, "Turkey in the Straw" on gleeful chimes,
and all the children came running, clutching coins
and then Fudgesicles, Dreamsicles, dripping cones,
and Bomb Pops, sunlight on their faces.

Birthday Cake

Always, birthday cake,
ice cream, and candles.

My mother saw to that.

When I was ten, I had my only party.
The kids got jump ropes as favors.

I got a Barbie with a bubble cut.
Her hair was platinum blonde.

We played on the jungle gym in the backyard.
I was the monkey bar queen.

In a photo I stand with my friends.
We are all smiles, wearing Madras shorts and pointy hats.

It was a happy day.

My mother saw to that.

~Southern Comfort Cake

—1 box yellow cake mix
—1 box (3 1/2 oz.) vanilla pudding
—4 eggs
—1/2 c. cold water
—1/2 c. oil
—1 c. chopped nuts
—1/2 c. Southern Comfort

Combine all in large bowl. Beat on medium speed for 2 minutes. Pour into a greased and floured Bundt pan or tube pan. Bake for one hour at 325 degrees. Set on rack to cool. Invert on serving plate. Prick top. Drizzle with 1/2 c. glaze (see below). Reheat remaining glaze and brush on cake. Sift 1 T. powdered sugar over cake. (Serves 12.)

Glaze
—4 T. softened butter
—1/8 c. water
—1/2 c. granulated sugar
—1/4 c. Southern Comfort

Beat together. Drizzle on half, then warm the rest and brush all over cake with a pastry brush.

The Thing About the Eye

    its fragility, its viscousness,
      the risks are many—tears or tears,
darkening, myopia, short-sightedness.

A girl in second grade wore thick glasses
    her last name was Tonatore.
Kids rhymed her name with *dinosaur.*

The "it" crowd in the back of the bus
    were the worst. The ride was long.

On weekends there were movie matinees.
    Black and brown kids sat in the theater balcony and poured Pepsi
      and popcorn on white kids down below.
No one thought much about it.
They wanted to see a movie or cartoon,
    the one where the mouse harasses the cat
      or the roadrunner flattens the coyote.

We knew very little,
    thought we were angels like those on holy cards.

I tried on my friend's glasses and everything went blurry.
    We didn't see much right in front of us.

Artichokes

Everything was a hand grenade
to my brothers who liked to play
war though we knew as children
of the sixties the horrors of My Lai,
napalm, one-armed vets. A pinecone
or an artichoke is not made of metal
and lacks a ring to detonate, a fuse
to ignite, explode, and fragment.

Once I tried to prepare artichokes
but was afraid of the spiny leaves,
the thistle, the choke, but when
the heart is bared, the soft core
bathed in oil, it's an aphrodisiac,
not an implement of destruction.
It melts as Cynara did in the arms
of Zeus who, jilted, flung her away
into the earth to emerge all spiny
and green, enclosing deep delight.

Callinectes Sapidus

In the green Chesapeake we trapped blue crabs
in wooden cages. The backstrokers clung
to chicken legs tied with kitchen twine.
Tugged from the brine, they dangled in sultry air
until dumped into baskets ridged with bailing wire.
Their carapaces turned red in boiling Old Bay broth.
Drained, the shelly bodies were sumptuous,
sun-tinged. We cracked the crabs with wooden mallets
on newspapered tables, popping the little purses
for mustard, orangey gonad, grabbing the gills
like feathered wings, the sand sac, juice down our arms.
We'd suck and slurp the meanest claw
holding the sweetest meat, best dipped
in malt vinegar or ramekins of butter.
This, a primer for how it was done
when we drove to the shore—the bay, a bountiful bowl
filled with savory beautiful swimmers.

~Crabmeat Dip

—8 oz. cream cheese
—1 T. milk
—1/2 t. horseradish
—6 1/2 oz. picked crabmeat, fresh is best
—dash pepper
—1/4 t. salt
—2 t. chopped onion
—1/2 c. slivered almonds

Combine all but the almonds. Put in baking dish. Sprinkle top with almonds. Bake at 375 for 15 minutes. Serve warm with crackers. (Serves 8-10.)

Kids

The high school playing field right behind
our home was our vista from a treehouse
where we saw Friday night football
beneath floodlights, cartwheeling cheerleaders,
purple and gold pom-poms, an all-star
wrestling exhibition with Haystacks Calhoun,
high school stragglers, smokers, cutting across.

Once my baby sister swallowed a Dum-Dum
and turned blue. I ran to the football field
and yelled to the crowd on the sidelines.
A man ran to our house, picked up Annie
and ran to his car. All that jiggling
made the sucker go down. No harm done.

Early summer we'd race across the empty field,
toss rocks from the tree towards the endzone;
late August, watch a quarterback run drills,
hear whistles like shrill birds.
Sweethearts made out beneath bleachers.

Some salvation in that field, the woods,
such as they were, trees thick with acorns,
our arboreal house, a haven and a crow's nest
overlooking a grassy sea, waves of teens,
swells of sound beneath a hunter's moon
we could almost touch in waning light

Carmen

"Your mother lets you wear make-up?" I ask
in awe of her radiance enhanced by applied color,
her hair, shimmering black.

"Can I borrow this bottle?" I ask,
which I do, but the color is Rachel, darkest shade,
that I apply to my face.
I become a pumpkin on an alabaster stalk.

At the bus stop they laugh behind their hands
at my strutting. Don't they see I'm Carmen,
don't they see my beauty?
My transformation?

In the girls' room in the trailer
that's our sixth-grade classroom,
I use Carmen's brilliant lipstick
like Picasso at his paints.

During spelling Sister Raymond pulls me
from my desk, drags me to the girls' room,
calls me a "strumpet,"
scrubs my face with woody paper towels.

With a warning about make-up Sister leaves me to
ablutions. In the mirror I am not Carmen
but a bleeding clown
staining the basin with Rachel-colored tears.

~Pumpkin Bread

—1 c. oil, canola or vegetable oil
—4 eggs
—2/3 c. water
—2 c. pumpkin puree
—3 c. sugar

—3 1/3 c. sifted flour
—2. t. soda
—1/2 t. salt
—1 t. cinnamon
—1 t. nutmeg

Mix oil, eggs, water, pumpkin, and sugar. Add in flour, soda, salt, cinnamon, and nutmeg. Grease two loaf pans. Divide batter between the two pans. Bake at 350 degrees for 60-70 minutes. Let cool a bit before removing. (Makes 2 loaves.)

Foreign Language

When my older sister took junior high French,
she taught me words here and there.
When we shopped in the Leggett's Ladies' Department,
we'd say these words so as to be overheard:

*Je suis fatigué; Qu'est-ce que c'est?; Où est l'école?;
Comment allez vous?; and Si'l vous plaît, mon petit choux.*

Lipsticked women wearing hats would think
we were foreign exchange students or exotics, world travelers.
How silly did we sound to keep asking
"Where is the school?" or "If you please, my little cabbage"?

After I took Spanish, we kept it up, repeating:

*¿Qué hay de almuerzo? Albondigas; ¿Qué tal, mi amiga?;
¿Quién es usted?; Buenos dias; Buenos tardes.*

When we rode bicycles downtown, we'd push them on the sidewalk,
making sure passersby heard us asking in Spanish: "What's for lunch?"
with the reply of "Meatballs" or querying, "What's up, friend?"

This was part of our conversation, memorized
for school skits and fill-in-the-blank tests.

How urbane and world weary in our plaid skirts, beanies, and blouses!
How we wished we could really be sophisticates, *mon petit choux, mi amiga!*

Berry Is My Madeleine

1. Once I ate a spider, brown like the dust-covered blackberry on which it sat. I popped it into my mouth then spit it out, crinkly spider legs twitching in twilight. In the distance, Monticello on a mountaintop, cement trucks passing on a gravel road. Davey and I crawled inside an abandoned cement truck barrel that made me claustrophobic but not like the time inside the St. Louis Arch, scrunched over, rising to the top, or in the Submarine Voyage at Disney Land, hatch locked, panic closing in. In the *Hunley*, the first submarine to sink a ship, men gripped and grappled with complicated wheels, turning a crank, firing a torpedo, dropping to the bottom, their chests, wild chambers. Their skeletons knock the ironsides, men still manning stations in the tidal pull.

2. When Sissy was put in the nursing home, she craved fresh fruit, specifically blueberries from a farm market down the street, big, round ones like tiny meatballs in a wedding soup. She'd overeat and get the runs but not like when she ate a whole bag of sugar-free Werther's candies. Sissy sang along with the Mennonites who came to evangelize and entertain the residents. "I got the Reese's Pieces, Reese's Pieces down in my heart, down in my heart, down in my heart" which was funnier than the peace that passeth understanding. She lost her faith when her four-year-old son Robin died from pneumonia. I read her an Emerson essay that said all good things are of God. She lost a lot of memory after a second heart attack and accidentally sipped from a coffee cup that held bacon grease. She thought her son Eric was building her a house near the family farm, his ploy to make her believe she could leave "the home."

3. My friend says she is a vegetarian but eats bacon. Mostly she eats peanut butter sandwiches, sometimes with boysenberry jam which wasn't a thing until Knott's Berry Farm crossed a blackberry, raspberry, and loganberry. Mama packed school lunches of peanut butter and jelly sandwiches, baloney sandwiches, or bacon sandwiches. I was embarrassed at the cafeteria table when I bit into rubbery bacon that flopped out onto my chin. In our family, the women hate their double chins and often take snapshots with their fists or flat hands beneath them, looking pensive. If you take a selfie, you are supposed to take it with the phone raised up. A lot of millennials take selfies. Some millennials plunged off a cliff near a waterfall in Yellowstone taking selfies. I'd like to take a selfie in a boysenberry patch, both red and black shiny fruit on the same bush, dangling like rubies from minty ears.

4. For Christmas this year, I would like a bayberry candle, which smells like spice and smoke. The wax from the berries smells like Christmas, like balsam

trees. In early December I drive out to Hampton to cut down a balsam. The aroma fills the truck. I wonder if baby Jesus liked the smell of frankincense and myrrh? There's a catalog company that sells a set of three candles labeled gold, frankincense, and myrrh. I wonder what the gold candle smells like? I've always liked spicy smells like apple cider with cinnamon simmering on the stove or Coco by Chanel. Clove gum used to be a thing. Smells can be warm too like a furry coat or a sheet right out of the dryer.

5. Hallie Berry's real first name is Maria. Her mother got her middle name, Hallie, from the name of a Cleveland department store. Her father abused her mother and hit her with a wine bottle. A boyfriend also hit Hallie, causing deafness in her left ear. She was the first African-American woman to win Best Actress for her role in *Monster's Ball* where she had a controversial nude scene with Billy Bob Thornton. As Catwoman, she received a Razzie for Worst Performance. Hallie plays Janie in *Their Eyes Were Watching God*. I like this strong woman in love with Tea Cake. Zora Neale Hurston wrote this novel about Eatonville, Florida. She also researched folk tales and was buried anonymously in a field until Alice Walker found her, these women, sweet like juice from a dark berry.

~Blueberry Muffins

—2 1/2 c. flour
—2 1/2 t. baking powder
—1 c. sugar
—1/4 t. salt
—1 c. shaken buttermilk
—2 eggs, beaten
—1/2 c. butter, melted in pan and slightly browned
—1 1/2 c. fresh blueberries

Grease 24 small muffin cups or line with paper cupcake liners. In a large bowl sift the dry ingredients. Make a well in the center and add buttermilk, beaten eggs, and slightly cooled browned butter. Mix well. Fold in blueberries. Fill muffin cups about 3/4 full. Bake in a 400-degree oven for 20 minutes. (Makes 24 small muffins.)

College Freshmen/Mountains

But I was afraid to make the leap
into the blue hole off the crag
like the daredevils in cut-off jeans
who jumped into the icy creek.

Into the blue hole off the crag
a darling boy and bikinied girl
who jumped into the icy creek
entered the shimmer, merely a swirl.

A darling boy and bikinied girl
the sun all around in blinking wonder
entered the shimmer, merely a swirl.
Friends held their breath in fear.

The sun all around in blinking wonder,
we shaded our eyes to see the feat.
Friends held their breath in fear.
We were all of seventeen.

We shaded our eyes to see the feat,
the plunge it was so deep.
We were all of seventeen,
wanting life and all it offered.

The plunge it was so deep,
but they emerged with a gulp of air,
wanting life and all it offered,
but I was afraid to make the leap.

Picking Asparagus

In early spring, tiny blades of green
cut through mudwash and mulch,
breaking through to form first hyacinths,
daffodils, and tulips. On the north
side of the mountain, three leaves
of ramps; along the roadside,
first thin spears of asparagus.
My sister and I pull the car over
to pick the spindles,
taking them home to blanch or roast
with oil, butter, lemon zest,
overeating since they were gratis,
bountiful. We spin them into grassy soup
dotted with sorrel or dill, a dollop
of sour cream, reliving consumption,
urine, sulfurous and rank,
but moods, elevated; bones,
stronger; energy, boosted enough
to dig in mud again, to forage for what is wild.

Meadows of Dan, Virginia

Leaf puzzle on the forest floor,
glass shine on a stalk,
a stream of milk, galax,
dotted with raindrops
near Mabry Mill that sluices
and shimmies water into runnels,
streams that turn the wheel
that run the grist
that grind the grain
to make hoe cakes or grits
with greasy beans once strung
on string to hang from beams
underneath where a blue tick
sleeps and snores, dreams
about treeing a ring tail
beneath a smoke moon
in the summer sky—
dear Lord, why would I
not smile? What should I
fear? The wheels are turning
even as we speak.

Where the River Ran

On the edge of Pawpaw's river property
stood a gnarled persimmon tree
we thought would wither and die
but green then gold flowers came.

The gnarled persimmon tree stood,
brought forth shiny-skinned fruit
from green then gold flowers fruit came
to gather after first sign of frost.

The shiny-skinned fruit came forth
enough for a wicker basketful
gathered after first frost,
sweetening the once-puckery fruit.

Enough for a wicker basketful,
enough to scoop out for pudding,
sweet now, this once-puckery fruit
gathered on Pawpaw's land.

The flesh scooped out for pudding
also good out of hand
gathered on Pawpaw's land
now cleared where the river ran.

The sweet of the fruit reminds me
of kin who have withered or died,
the loss of a family legacy,
the loss of Pawpaw's property.

Grandmothers North and South

One grandmother made *ponczki*; one, piccalilli,
a yeasty Polish donut and Southern relish, respectively,
foods in their DNA connected to culture, home,
treats for Fat Tuesday or a breakfast side
with eggs over easy, grits, streak o' lean.

Grandma's arthritic hands kneaded dough,
punched it down, pulled it apart, inoculated puffs with jam,
sprinkled sugar like January snow.

The back of Mamaw's arms jiggled, stirring a pot of peppers,
onions, green tomatoes redolent with spices, vinegar, sugar,
Mason jars on tea towels, pinging to seal.

Grandma, Minnesota-born, married Frank
off the Mississippi levee. He tippled whisky and blacked her eye.
To escape, she baked, grew snapdragons, tended a house on Magnolia Street.

Mamaw, Shenandoah Valley-bred and educated, married Harvey,
dough boy, farmer, ship builder, chugger of Pabst. She begat ten kids,
cooked and scrimped to survive, the root cellar potato cold.

We grandchildren worshiped at the altars of these women
and received holy offerings at Formica tables.
Their chalice cloths were paper napkins.
Our eyes glittered like stars. Our mouths, too full to pray.

Ponczki   (Makes About 50)
1 pt. milk----3 eggs---1½ cups sugar
1 yeast cake---½ cup butter or half butter
half lard---1 tsp. salt---1 tsp. vanilla or
rind of orange--- flour to make soft dough
Heat ½ milk with butter, add a little milk to
yeast to dissolve, put aside. In large bowl
put heated milk; let cool add rest of milk,
sugar, salt, 2 cups flour, beat well, separate
eggs, beat yolks, add to mixture, add 1 cup flour,
add vanilla and yeast, 2 cups flour, add stiffly
beaten egg whites to mixture, and enough flour
to make a soft dough, like for coffe cake.
Make in morning, let rise double. Deep fry
till done, about 9 minutes.

My grandmother's original recipe

Avocados/Father

Rasps, roads, sandpaper—
rough or bumpy,
ridged or rutted, tough on the thumb
like an avocado, alligator pear,
peel like reptilian scutes
or aging skin
benefited by avocado
oil, unctuous flesh
spooned out, smashed
and smeared onto toast,
new-age breakfast,
a-drip with tined lemon
and lime, Tabasco,
for a guacamole tang.

My father had an outer toughness
tempered by a yielding heart
not like a stony seed—
more like an ooze of cherry cordial
or milky gush from coconut,
softness evident upon breaking,
which hearts do,
though they can turn hard
after being bruised, mishandled.

An avocado cradles a core
when suspended in water
sprouts fresh tendrils
to begin life anew.

A human heart stops forever.

~Guacamole

—2 medium very ripe avocados
—2 medium ripe tomatoes
—1 small onion, grated
—2 small hot chilies, chopped, or dash of chili powder
—dash of paprika

—1 T. olive oil
—2 t. (1 of each) lime and lemon juice
—2 t. salt or to taste
—1/2 t. ground coriander

Mash avocados. Stir in other ingredients to a lumpy consistency. Serve with tostadas, chips, or crackers. (Makes 3 cups.)

Apples/Father

I've bought into the adage about eating an apple a day
like my father who hated going to the doctor,
who'd do anything to avoid the cost, the white coats,
but suffered for it with "spells," as folks
used to call them, which eventually killed him.

The crunch of an apple satisfies,
all that white flesh and juice, sometimes
even better chopped and resting
under a bed of oats, brown sugar, and butter,
an autumn crisp, or melting under a layer
of wheaty flour and lard, the all-American pie
served with a wedge of cheddar
or a scoop of ice cream dotted
with vanilla flecks like so many freckles.

Doctors forbid all that dairy fat and refined sugar
and prefer the fruit naked like Eve
who took that first bite and tempted Adam
which did not turn out so well,
the serpent having his way, God's abandonment,
Eve condemned to labor pains.

Maybe it was a Pink Lady or some special
hybrid called Knowledge that made the first woman
subject to man's criticism and abuse to this day.

And here I started so well, daddy and apples on my mind.

~Granny's Apple Pie

—apples (about eight)
—lemon juice from half of a lemon
—2 pie crusts, your favorite
—3/4 to 1 c. sugar depending on tartness of apples
—1 t. cinnamon
—1 t. nutmeg
—1 t. ginger
—3 T. butter
—2-3 T. flour

Preheat oven to 450. Slice enough apples in a bowl to fill a pie pan full, about eight. Sprinkle apples with lemon juice. Mix cinnamon, nutmeg, ginger, and flour together. Sprinkle all of the seasonings, including sugar, over 3 layers of apples, but do not put sugar on the top layer. Dot with butter. Cover with top crust, seal, and flute. Bake at 450 for 15 minutes and at 425 for 45 minutes. (Serves 8.)

Apricots
inspired by Inger Christensen's Alphabet

Apricots exist
on a Sèvres plate
near a tumble of grapes,
still life painted,
or on a tree laden,
dropping soft fruit
collected in baskets
by bakers to layer
for tarts or stewed
for great aunts
who slip children
five-dollar bills,
who sip creme de menthe,
who sit in corners at reunions,
smiling and nodding,
deaf as codfish,
adjusting spectacles
to read birthday cards,
hugging with crackling
bones, limping out
to the car, smiling
behind the back window
behind a child's handprint
wet with apricot juice.

~Apricot Chicken with Almonds

—4 six-ounce skinless boneless chicken breast halves
—1/2 and 1/8 t. salt
—1/2 t. black pepper
—1/3 c. sliced almonds
—1/2 c. apricot preserves
—1 1/2 T. soy sauce
—1 T. whole-grain mustard
—1 T. unsalted butter

Put oven rack in lower third of oven and preheat oven to 400 degrees. Lightly oil a 12"x 9" flameproof baking dish (not glass). Pat chicken dry with paper towels. Sprinkle all over with 1/2 teaspoon salt and 1/4 teaspoon pepper total, then arrange at least 1/4 inch apart in baking dish. Bake 10 minutes. While chicken bakes, toast almonds in a small baking pan in oven, stirring twice, until golden, 8 to 10 minutes. Watch carefully because they burn easily.

Cook apricot preserves, soy sauce, mustard, butter, and 1/8 teaspoon salt and 1/4 teaspoon pepper in a small saucepan over moderate heat, stirring, until preserves are melted. Pour sauce over chicken and continue to bake until chicken is just cooked through, about 10 minutes more. Turn on broiler and broil chicken 4 to 5 inches from heat, basting once until chicken is glazed and browned in spots, about 3 minutes. Serve sprinkled with almonds. (Serves 4.)

Mist

In the middle of Wexford, Ireland,
eating strawberries wet from washing,
I heard my mother call my name from hills
dotted with rock and nodding cattle
lying down, waiting for rain.

It must have been fairies
crawled out of their fairy mound
or a leprechaun versed in mimicry
in imitation of her voice
since she had left for good the year before.

It could have been the hills themselves that spoke,
but in the middle of Wexford,
she clearly said my name.

I turned to look for her
but only saw purple rhododendrons,
spikes of loosestrife,
a misty morning,
Wicklow Mountains in the distance.

—Strawberry Jell-O Salad

—two 6-oz. packages of strawberry Jell-O (you also can use raspberry)
—3. c. boiling water
—1 20-oz. can crushed pineapple, drained
—two-10-oz. packages of frozen strawberries, sweetened or unsweetened (you can also use raspberries)
—two soft mashed bananas
—2 t. fresh lemon juice
—1 c. sour cream

Dissolve Jell-O in boiling water. Add frozen berries, mashed bananas, pineapple, and lemon juice. Pour half of this mixture in a container of your choice and let set for about 15 minutes in the refrigerator. Keep the other half at room temp. Watch both carefully because they set up quite quickly. When the refrigerated Jell-O is set, or almost set, frost with 1 c. sour cream, and spread the other half of the Jell-O on top. Refrigerate until fully set.

Off

    This afternoon I listen for the pop
        of the pickle jars
            to ensure their sealed lives.

    Outside a yellowjacket bores into a hole
        on the hummingbird feeder
            and flies out of another.

    Nothing enters that isn't allowed.

    On my hands and knees,
        like my mother
            used to do,
    I wash the floor,
            scraping grit out of the corner
                with a fingernail.

    The rocking chair moves back and forth.
        Someone sees my fear
            boiling over, dousing flame.

    We are afraid of everything and nothing.

        Outside I chop into arterial weeds
            that invade my garden
                and warily watch a bat
                    suckered to the wall.

~Watermelon Pickles

-salted water to cover
—rind from 1/2 a watermelon, cut up in chunks

—2 c. sugar
—1 c. water
—1 c. vinegar
—1 cinnamon stick
—8 cloves (without heads)

Peel off dark green and pink from a half watermelon. Soak rind in salty water overnight in refrigerator. The next day, boil rind 10-15 minutes in the water. Boil syrup separately: sugar, water, vinegar, cinnamon stick, and cloves 10 minutes and add just the rind. Cook until rind turns clear. Pour pickles and juice into a couple of clean quart jars (depends on size of melon). Seal and sterilize in hot boiling water, about ten minutes.

Gardening
inspired by "Mary, Mary, Quite Contrary," traditional

Why the face, dear Mary, fire in your eyes?
Why the wistful look, clouds and clouds of sighs?

After hard work, the watering can,
the seeds, the soil, a carefully laid plan,
silly things sprout day after day—
silver bells with no nutrition,
cockleshells that have arisen,
empty, devoid of edible flesh,
pretty maids I cannot thresh,
providing no grain or succulent fruit,
silky slippers in place of roots.
They laugh at me, these coquettes,
displacing all the onion sets,
dancing upon slender stalks,
listening to the farmers talk.
And so, the garden, lovely in its way,
gives me no pleasure, only dismay
that I have no baskets full of food,
that what I have planted does no good
except in nursery rhymes and fanciful tales
about inedible plants, crops that fail.

Worry, Worry, Worry

Courage cannot be plucked like fruit
from a vine. It's not as easy as taking
a bite of fennel or a glumph of spinach.

It's not just the Cowardly Lion's list though
it can make a king out of a slave,
it can make a flag to wave.

I'd like to face mad dogs or formless monsters
instead of slipping down rabbit holes.

I'd like to impale fears on a spike until
it resembled a spiny sea urchin, then skip
outside, hurl it like a ninja star
toward the moon.

Fears would go away if I could have
solitude like Yeats in his *bee-loud glade*,
Rumi's silence inside growing roots.

I'd banish electronic hysteria
and listen to the hum of the world.

The Waczieleski Girls

Bernice, Dolores, Margie, white hair like knitted caps,
owl-eyed spectacles, cravings for York Peppermint Patties,
get together to reminisce. Outside, rain fills a swollen stream.
Great-Aunt Bernice leans into a walker
like she leaned into life, bent now, intrepid.
Bernice likes apples peeled and sliced
in a baggie she places in a flowered sack
tied to her walker. She mentions loving walleye
and red salmon right out of the can.
She remembers everyone, even at 93.
Dolores, my grandmother, sits next to Bernice
and stares, a Styrofoam cup in her hand.
Her eye sparks silver with an intraocular lens.
She turned 89 in December and remembers it will be three
years May 29 that my mother, her eldest, died.
Although it is May 28, she tells me to have a nice
Christmas. She announces that her youngest
had a heart attack. My Aunt Kathy corrects,
"Mom, Mike never had a heart attack."
I speak loudly, "Doesn't he have an irregular heart beat?"
Grandma looks blank, Lewy body dementia taking hold.
Great-Aunt Margie in a Walmart pants suit brings her sisters
hard candy and slippers. She crochets as she converses.
She gets around with husband Ed to the casino
for nickel slots and to Kohl's on a bus.
Dolores was always jealous of her youngest sister:
Margie got to finish school. Margie always had good health.
Margie has been married for 64 years. Margie was never abused.
I would like to raise these women up to beauteous light,
to strong limbs and eyes that still see dimes hiding
in corners. I would like to pour them cold water to refresh
parched lips and throats that emit whispery words like
fine-grained sandpaper. I would like to send cool breezes
to fan their feverish foreheads, to warm blankets
to drape over their folded shoulders. To take
their hands and rub them into circulation.
To be a life line in the dark water that rises in spring.

Salmon

Some of the flesh is gray, soft,
purply where mercury lies.
This is carved away,
scraped into a pulpy mash
pushed to the side of the platter.

We needle nose pin bones like slivers of moon,
eat the remaining silky filets,
pure protein, fatty, amino acids.

Good fat from the coldest sea
oils the rusty parts,
the fish unknowingly giving us
memories we never want to lose.

We sleep in blue currents of our own.

~Marinated Salmon in Pepper Crust

—2 T. soy sauce
—1 large garlic clove, mashed
—2 t. fresh lemon juice
—1 t. sugar
—3/4 lb. salmon fillet, skinned and cleaned
—4 t. coarsely ground black pepper
—2 T. olive oil

In plastic bag or dish, combine first four ingredients for marinade. Marinate salmon for 30 minutes or up to a couple of hours. Pat slightly dry with paper towels. Press pepper onto moist fish. Coat thoroughly. In heavy skillet (preferably cast iron), heat olive oil over moderately high heat until hot. Sauté the salmon two minutes each side or until fish flakes with a fork. Drain on paper towel. (Caution: Turn on fan because the pepper fumes can make you sneeze.)

Good with a rice pilaf or white rice. (Serves 2.)

Reasons to Survive October
after Tony Hoagland's "Reasons to Survive November"

October like a mellow friend
bearing vintage wine and aged cheese
has crept in on soft-soled shoes,
washing canvases with golden
fire, tingeing tangerine rugose leaves.

Driving to Cub Grocery for pitted dates,
hothouse cukes, I nearly crash into a curb,
startled by incarnadine sumac
aflame on the edge of the road.

Later, in the backyard,
turkeys are black hands folded in prayer,
                              egrets like handkerchiefs.

The vegetable garden is gnarled and brown,
but the tomatoes are still shiny green
                              on blighted vines.

These will be a mock apple pie,
all cinnamon and ooze,
the smell of the woodlands,
desperate vegetation.

I don't like to say good-bye
to my brisk, beautiful friend.
After she leaves, her sister
brings dead things, cold and dark.

Distant Lightning
an elegy for John Hagstrom

All day rain fell. A song on the radio, a perfect alignment
with melancholy, yet a rock lobster jouncing
across my sensibility brought you up,
my friend, in joyous puffs. Colorado bulldog
in hand, smoke rings overhead, tow-headed
in bibbed jeans on a summer night, the night
the Northrop balcony swayed to "Love Shack,"
Dancin' Johnny, rainbow farmer, bang bang on the floor,
the balcony barely moored to plaster.
We exited to rain-slicked streets, arm-in-arm
near Lind Hall. At Chester's, you fried Monte Cristos
as crisp as the ruffled toque you wore.
Mini-donuts at Taste of Minnesota, five years,
slinging yellow dough into hoppers, reefer
in the port-a-potty, cold Coronas on ice. Spatula mad,
you cooked for kings, basting T-bones, serving drag queens
in old St. Paul houses wall-papered with your art. One of our last
times together, cheesy chips, salsa in sombrero bowls,
rain spattering strung lights. Somehow we lost touch
but found each other at the mall. You slathered butter on pastry
for Cinnabons tucked like crowns inside paper boxes,
your eye-rolling boredom evident. I bumped into you
at Restoration Hardware, looking at faux school lights with Jason,
your true love who left you bereft, back to his former life,
two kids and a wife from Fargo. Was it white Russians?
A party *every* night? Rendezvous in dark bars. When we pretended
to be the Golden Girls, you were always Blanche,
an AIDS cocktail socked down with a screwdriver.
Your voice scraped the air, so many screams into your pillow.
No one bothered to tell me your sister found you
bleeding from the mouth on the white tile polished with Bon Ami,
your Japanese robe loose over a bloated tummy, your head bruised,
parents never accepting, even in death, their only son,
those good Swedes safe in suburbia with their Schnoodle, and you,
cherry tree dweller by a stream, singing at the top of your lungs,
"It's the end of the world as we know it. I feel fine!", lightplay
in gelled hair, blue eyes snapping with flecks of gold,
one-hooped ear, beneath a disco ball. Electricity in the air,

the line gone dead, an unacknowledged sympathy card, hot tears
until you float like Moses down the swollen river of your life,
whirling in eddies others stirred around you, Dancin' Johnny,
hydroplaning into another dimension, *tin roof, rusted.*

Circle Dance

Mini donut batter, a gooey yellow ribbon, follows the spatula lifted from a giant bowl. It's an easy recipe: two parts premade mix to one part water by weight. Hefting the bowl, the chef pours the batter into gallon pitchers then into the Lil' Orbits'™ hopper. The cutter drops four perfect little O's into melted shortening, which float down a river of grease, errant inner tubes, flipped twice by metal flippers until they tumble into a pan. The golden O's pile up. High school girls scoop them into paper bags that spot with grease, sprinkle cinnamon and sugar, and shake, shake, shake. The festival crowd grows googly-eyed, waiting for hot, fresh donuts.

O

I work so long and hard, I dream of donuts spewing endlessly out of machinery, going wild, shooting across the sky, turning into flying saucers filled with aliens who, for some reason, eschew the sugary treat and munch on pretzels stacked in snack bowls scattered about the ship. All is chaos as planets careen and whiz about, meteors ablaze, and we're back beneath the tent, stringing little O's into bracelets that burn our arms, leaving welts and streaks of red.

O

O's are everywhere—the bone ring of the eye socket, a wedding band, a bicycle tire, a button, a halo. A baby's chin sports a wayward Cheerio. At the end of *Catcher in the Rye,* Phoebe rides a carousel, Holden weeping. My brother picks a perfect oxeye daisy. Kindergartners link construction paper rings for Christmas. An O-ring creates a seal in a water pipe. The Lakota dancer weaves through colorful hoops. Jackie O was a gracious first lady. Pepperoni dots a cheesy pizza. O stands for Oprah.

O

The work crew is pleased when they see the perfect O's, but, when the cutter goes dry, the batter oozes figure 8s. Tiny pieces break and burn in the hot oil. Dripping dough churns out blobs, damming the stream as flippers labor to toss deformations. The machine operator lifts the hopper away from the burning bath and unclogs the cutters. With greasy fingers, he lubricates the cutting edge. After a few false starts, the machine, once again, pumps out fluffy O's.

O

In my youth, I stretched linen taut clamped into a hoop to embroider hearts and flowers, sentiments of love. My mother was a better seamstress, impossibly darting A-line shifts, working with bunched velvet beneath her fingertips. She died before her time, a rare leukemia. Finding a blood match for O negative was part of the problem. She died before her time.

O

The O explains death—from womb to tomb—like the opening song of *The Lion King* "The Circle of Life." In the Buddhist mandala, the deity sits at the center of the O, source of light. The sick sit in the middle of Navaho healing circles. Tibetan monks sketch sand paintings whose central figure is the O. One is always trying to center one's self with the center of the universe. As years pass, more people within one's circle die.

O

Mini donuts will morph into imperfect O's if the chef screws up the mix to water ratio. If the batter is too runny, the donuts form 6s as they plop from the hopper, running together in a continental mass. If the batter is too thick, the donuts become dense balls sporting slight indentations like belly buttons. Bobbing like otter heads, they roll in the oily stream. Low batter level produces thin, hard, crunchy donuts that fry to a darkish brown like bad onion rings.

O

O is the omicron, the 15th letter of the alphabet. Placed before a noun, it is a vocative: O My Papa! O Canada! O Solitude! O Captain My Captain! Paired with an h, is an interjection: "Oh my goodness!" "Oh dear!" or a preposition sans *f*: "Top o' the mornin'! or will-o'-the wisp. O is our surprise, our joy, our shock, our sorrow. " O O O O that Shakespeherian Rag!" O's symbolize cycle, endlessness, ouroboros. Native Americans camp in circles. Birds weave circular nests. Sumerians organized time according to circular bounds, echoes of sun dials, clocks, and watches. The O is God, the alpha and the omega, completeness in both time and space.

O

As the day wanes, bags of surplus donuts are sold cheaply or given away, disintegrating on tongues like greasy communion wafers. Inside the tent, tiny O's stick to the bottoms of shoes. Burnt and disfigured O's are tossed into a waste basket. A full moon illuminates a distant Ferris wheel. We bring the car around for our trip back home. *Wheel in the sky keeps on turning.*

~Donuts

—2 eggs
—1 c. sugar
—1/2 c. milk
—2 1/2 c. flour
—3 t. baking powder
—1/2 t. salt
—1/4 t. mace or nutmeg
—1/2 t. vanilla
—shortening

Beat eggs well. Sift in sugar; beat well. Add milk and stir in dry ingredients; mix well. Add vanilla. Add more flour if needed (dough should not be soft); pat dough into thickness wanted on floured surface; cut in circles and fry in hot shortening (350 degrees) so they float; turn as needed to brown and drain on paper; let cool. Optional: Shake on powdered sugar or sugar/cinnamon mix (Yield: about one dozen)

On Blindness

I am no Milton who accepted blindness
or Borges who took to aural beauty after
he could no longer see his golden tigers.
Poets need vision, the real kind, to see
raindrops on panes, a fluttering cloud
of monarchs, colors, a lover's eyes.

An ocular exam reveals a darkening on the bottom
of my right eye, blindness for peripheral things,
a glaucomic erasure. All my life it seems
I've worn glasses, a groove on the bridge
of my nose. No change even after eating carrots
and veggies high in beta carotene.
Visual field tests scare me. What if I don't see
that pinprick of light? When I was young,
spectacles were cool especially John Lennon wire rims.
I often tried on friends' glasses
though my mother warned me not to.

Vision is precious. When the blind
suddenly see whether because of Jesus
or surgery they cry when swirling colors
morph into the faces of their loved ones,
majestic trees, an arcing rainbow.
They cry and then look at everything
with a poet's eyes
for the very first time.

~Glazed Carrot Packet

—1 sheet (18"x 24") aluminum foil
—1 package (16 ounces) peeled baby carrots
—1/3 c. orange marmalade
—1/4 c. packed brown sugar
—1/2 ground cinnamon
—1 T. butter

Preheat oven to 450 degrees or preheat grill to medium-high. Center carrots on sheet of aluminum foil. Combine marmalade, brown sugar and cinnamon and spread over carrots. Top with butter or margarine. Bring up sides of foil and double fold top and sides to form one large foil packet, leaving room for heat circulation inside packet. Bake for 25 to 30 minutes on a cookie sheet in oven or grill 15 to 20 minutes in a covered grill. (Serves 4.)

The Art of Hearing

Used to be I could hear a pin drop or a student whispering
in the back of a classroom, despite heater fan, hallway
chatter, band practices, planes overhead.
Now I have to look pretty much directly at a speaker's
face, preferably a close talker. Forget about understanding
hollered tidbits from another room, something people
tend to do especially if I am washing dishes,
water running, or in the laundry room, the whoosh
of washer in my ears, or in the bathroom,
door closed, Sonic toothbrush buzzing in my head.
A yeller from another room might as well be saying
"rutabaga, rutabaga, rutabaga," or intoning the thespian
crowd sound of "rhubarb, rhubarb, rhubarb."

When I make dinner reservations with elderly relatives,
I request a quiet corner away from piped-in music
or a clattering kitchen. Even with hearing aids
it's always, "What?"; "Excuse me?";
"I'm sorry, what did you say?"; "Huh?"
Those with hearing appliances often talk softly,
so I too must ask for conversation
to be repeated or lean in as if for a kiss.

I like to hear the world but likely heard it too loudly
as a young person paying no heed to the reverb
on a guitar, cranking up Hendrix or Zeppelin
on the stereo headphones or eight-track deck.

I still like loud rock and roll—after all, it *is* rock and roll.
It's hard to appreciate a muffled Jimmy Page riff
or a distant Patrick Carney drum-thumping.
They might as well be playing from Jupiter
or mumbling something about root vegetables.

~Rhubarb Crisp

—1 c. flour —1/2 to 3/4 c. slightly soft margarine or butter
—5 T. powdered sugar

Cut together and mix well. Pat into a 9" pan. Bake for 15 minutes at 350 degrees - don't overcook.

—2 beaten eggs
—1 1/4 c. sugar
—1 c. flour
—1/2 t. baking powder
—2 c. rhubarb (finely chopped)
—1/2 t. baking powder

Mix together eggs, sugar, flour, baking powder; then mix in rhubarb and pour over baked crust. Bake for 30 minutes at 350 degrees. (Serves 6.)

Teeth

My brother's teeth are so white, they nearly blind me. In a dark photo he looks like the Cheshire Cat. Daddy used to give me a stiff toothbrush and tell me to brush the yellow away. Chinese women used to dye their teeth with eggplant skin to darken them. A dentist told me teeth are rarely bright white with shades of gray and yellow being common. Having teeth of any color is better than the alternative. My grandmother on my father's side only had two teeth and gummed her food. My grandfather on my mother's side used to scare the grandkids with his extracted false teeth, clacking them like castanets. Several of my aunts and uncles had partials or uppers or lowers, sometimes painful or oozing Polydent. I have four bridges to span gaps and to repair a snaggletooth I broke twice, once on my sister's head in a game of leap frog and once on a Nehi bottle jiggled in a car ride. If you dream about losing teeth, you are probably anxious, beginning something new, worried about aging, health, or being attractive to the opposite sex, or, as some cultures believe, soon to lose a family member. I have finally accepted my teeth, gaps, color, and all, having trepidations about times spent in dental chairs upside down, gagging on goo or molds, appreciative but uncomfortable with scraping or drilling. Since I eschew farina, gruel, or pap, this will be done.

Falling Down

Family and friends as of late tell of
people falling, results of Parkinson's,
weak backs, inattention to surroundings, a cluttered
or slippery environment, home or outdoors.

In the 1800s a paucity of public trashcans
gave rise to rotting banana peel litter,
bananas being a common on-the-go snack.
"Sliding" Billy Watson, the first comedian
to use the banana-peel-slip gag, glided on the stage
for a laugh but got a bigger one when he fell.

Once I set a magazine on the steps
but forgot about it, so, when running downstairs
for the phone, I slipped on a glossy picture
of Rihanna, landing on my coccyx bone,
which wasn't funny though the bone's name is.

The modern equivalent of a banana peel
just might be the distraction of a cell.
People with eyes glued to screens may smack
into walls or poles, fall into holes, fly into traffic,
or step into a fountain, hitting their head on a gargoyle.
They *might* even slip on a blackened banana peel.

It's not funny when someone slips and falls.
What we really want is sure footing
wherever we go, balance on this earth.

~Banana Cake

—2 1/2 c. flour
—1 1/2 c. sugar
—1 1/2 t. baking powder
—1 t. baking soda
—1 t. salt

—1/2 c. shortening
—3 mashed ripe bananas
—2/3 c. buttermilk
—1 t. vanilla
—2 eggs

Grease and lightly flour 9 x 13 cake pan. Combine flour, sugar, baking powder, baking soda, and salt. Mash bananas and add vanilla in separate bowl. Add this mixture with shortening to the flour mixture. Beat on low speed with electric mixer until combined. Add eggs and buttermilk. Beat 2 min. on medium speed. Turn batter into pan. Bake at 350 degrees for 30 min. or until middle springs back.

Frosting
- —6 T. softened butter
- —4 1/2 c. powdered sugar
- —1 1/2 t. vanilla
- —1 pasteurized egg

Mix together and then beat well. Add milk if needed for consistency. (Serves 12)

What's Been Taken Away

When a hostess set out a salad of citrus,
I had to pick around the grapefruit,
spooning up kiwi and mandarin oranges.
I had to turn down the salty dog proffered in a cabana.
A box of Christmas grapefruit sent from Florida
went untouched, buzzed by fruit flies.

I crave grapefruit though now *verboten* since Atorvastatin.
Truth be told, I wasn't mad about it unless coated in sugar,
scored to prevent a caustic squirt to the eye,
segmented into suprémes.

I'm like the rebellious teen who chugged Boone's Farm,
wanting what's not allowed.
I long for a Ruby Red in a white bowl,
forbidden fruit, a Barbados wonder, especially since,
like sex on an airplane, I can't.

~Mandarin Orange Salad

—1/4 c. slivered almonds
—2 T. sugar

To caramelize almonds, heat almonds and sugar in a small frying pan or saucepan over medium heat until sugar melts & nuts turn a light brown, stirring constantly. Be very careful: These burn easily. Remove from heat and continue to stir. Turn out onto a greased cookie sheet or pie pan (or sheet of aluminum foil) to cool.

—1 bunch of romaine lettuce (recommend a couple of romaine hearts, chopped)
—1 c. chopped celery
—2 green onions with tops, chopped
—1 (11-oz) can mandarin oranges, drained

Dressing:
—1/4 c. (canola or a light) oil
—2 T. (rice wine) vinegar
—2 T. sugar
—1/2 t. salt
—A few dashes of Tabasco sauce
—pepper to taste

Shake in a jar and set aside at room temperature.

To make the salad: Toss together the romaine, celery, green onions, and mandarin oranges. Pour the dressing over the greens, no more than 1/2 hour before serving or the lettuce will wilt. Add the caramelized almonds. (Serves 4-6.)

Italy, Late December

In Rosignole, the locals shop
in the market for New Year's,
the Mediterranean catch, so fresh,
an eel slivers over crushed ice.

Shrimp wave celebratory feelers
by the silver sardines.
"Buon ano! Buon feste!" marketers call.
A pig's head smiles beneath sprouted hairs.

Red and green tomatoes glisten
like Christmas lights near gigantic peppers
bereted men weigh. In the deli, wheels of crusty
bread are stacked into towers.

The server intones a litany:
"Mortadella, capicola, salami, prosciutto."
When we leave, we choose jumbo gelatos,
stroll and whisper like true Tuscans.

Here we are in a new year,
ancient olive trees gnarled on the sides of mountains.
Rain clouds gather over palm trees.
In the distance, the sea.

Let us kiss and remember this moment,
this sacred soil on which we stand.
Bella Toscana, you enchant us,
we who have let first fires die.

After Reading Bukowski

He came to me a little drunk, smiling,
and bent me back for a long, grizzled kiss.
I found him rough, but manly, beguiling,
so melted in his arms, hirsute bliss.
Soon he grew thirsty—he wanted a Schlitz,
opened the fridge, saw my green celery boat
filled with shrimp salad so he had a bit
but a little hard shell stuck in his throat.
Just then my husband walked in the back door,
saw old Buk picking shrimp from stained teeth.
He assessed the scene, pushed him to the floor,
mayo-covered prawns stuck to his feet.
Slowly Charles rose, coughed, lit a bidi,
offered hubby one—didn't want to be greedy.

Change of Heart

He used to have the heart of a grizzly
pumping blood of love, compassion, magnanimity,
summer red and rapid.

Is it something about getting older, forgetting
the role of the limbic, the cardiovascular?

Is it the weather?

Likely, it's the lack of a good night's sleep,
the need for a rare roast beef.

Creature comforts take precedence
like a sleepy Kodiak
waiting for the fattest salmon to leap into his mouth
or chewing on an abandoned kill
still flopping onshore, his dried cranberry heart
fluttering in a hollow, roars catching in his throat.

~Overnight Beef Roast

—6 pounds of sirloin tip "rolled" roast beef
—2 packages dried Lipton onion soup (can use less)
—2 jars Heinz mushroom gravy
—1 c. Wishbone Italian dressing
—2 cans drained mushrooms

Place roast in large roasting pan. Mix onion soup, mushroom gravy, 1 cup Italian dressing, and 2 cans drained mushrooms. Pour over roast. Roast in covered pan 3 hours at 350 degrees. Chill overnight. Next day, slice roast thinly and place in casserole. Skim fat from gravy and pour gravy over meat. Reheat in covered dish up to 1 hour at 350 degrees. (Serves 12.)

To Prepare and Care

Potatoes pared and quartered
will belch and buckle, unattended on the stove.

The elderberry's stem bores deep into the fruit
and must be singly plucked.

Baked Alaska takes time and talent,
all that sponge, meringue, and fire.

Hourly Mama skimmed scum and nitrates
from the tub water that held a country ham.

And what about this heart under pressure,
its purple core bruised and stabbed
like a fist clutching wet nettles?

Its need for attentive care?

What about it?

Till Death Do Us Part

After the long walks,
some, hand-in-hand,

after the installment of dishwashers,
shower heads, ballcocks, finials,

after eggs and potatoes, kebabs,
beet salads with goat cheese,

after nostalgia replaces reality,
after coolness on the couch,

after tiptoeing in the rain
to fetch the paper,

after all of this,
here we are,

a loop of television news,
brandy-laced fruitcake,
coffee rings in the sink,

sinus medicine,
cancer scares,

counterpoint to quiet,
nose to nose

in a goodish way,
snow silently building a wall.

~Dad's Fruitcake

Part I
Grease with butter eight standard loaf pans or 18 little aluminum loaf pans and line with wax paper, trimming edges. Store in refrigerator.
—1 lb., 12 oz. soft butter
—1 lb., 12 oz powdered sugar (almost 8 cups, unsifted)

—1/8 t. soda
—1 t. salt

—1/8 t. cream of tartar
—2 lbs., 2. oz. flour (8 c. unsifted, then sift)
—14 large eggs

Cream the butter, powdered sugar, soda, and salt. Then mix everything together. (Use a very big bowl and a hand mixer.)

Part II

—1 T. vanilla

—1/2 c. water

—3 lbs. bleached raisins

—2. lbs. candied green and red cherries cut in half

—1 lb., 4 oz. candied or dried pineapple cut in chunks

—20 oz. pecans or walnuts, barely chopped

Add fruit and nuts to the first mixture, saving some fruit and whole nuts for a garnish on top. Fill pans about 3/4 full and garnish. Be sure the pans are cold, greased lightly, and lined with waxed paper. Batter will be very thick. Make an egg wash out of 1 egg and a little water and beat well. Pat onto batter, pushing batter well into corners. Bake at 275 for 2 to 2 1/2 hours. Color should be golden brown.

Part III

After the cakes are cool, remove from pans and remove waxed paper from cakes. Take a piece of cheesecloth and dip into beverage of choice (whiskey, rum, or brandy.). Wrap cake with soaked cheesecloth and wrap tightly in foil. Cloth should be refreshed every week. Better aged for at least one month.

(My mother inherited this recipe from her father who was a baker by profession. When she began baking the fruitcake, the results were not perfect because the instructions were slightly vague. She had to experiment and ask him for more directions. We benefit from what are about five years' refinements to the Christmas recipe. No doorstops in this batch.)

On the Groaning Board

Tiny Tim asks his sister Martha if she would like to hear the pudding sing in the kettle, and since it is Christmas, I assume it is a figgy pudding. Some call it plum pudding though it has neither plums nor figs. It does have raisins and currants. This is not your Jell-O pudding. It stands up straight like a Cossack's hat and is crowned with a sprig of holly. Its traditional 13 ingredients represent Christ and his apostles. Jesus gets in on a lot of holiday food. Consider King Cake or a hot cross bun. Figs are actually quite sexual, both vulvic and phallic. Is it because Adam and Eve wove the leaves into clothes to cover their nether regions? The fig tree symbolizes the Greek god Priapus, and we all know what a randy fellow he was. I'd like to taste a figgy pudding one day, watch it go up in flames, awash in brandy, but I hear it can be a tad heavy. Anything that makes people not go until they get some has to have some redeeming qualities.

Early October 2020

An orange-tinged finch brings friends
to the feeder, four others like bright candles
alighting near potted herbs and green onions.

They are my only guests lately.

I've boxed up the good china, candlesticks,
given away an ice cream maker, a bread machine,
thumbed through myriad cookbooks.

Tonight it's catfish fingers and fried green tomatoes,
what's in the freezer, what needs to be used.

Sometimes we gather in parks, weather permitting,
by the Mississippi, in backyards, distancing,
masks at the ready. We reminisce about wood-paneled
steakhouses, dinner parties with cloth napkins,
Barolos, something flambéed

We miss greetings, hugs, full-out guffaws.

We miss poetry readings, the theater, live music.

We settle for PBS, Kraft mac and cheese,
Zoom screens like *Brady Bunch* boxes.

In the sky, finches fly.

Sugar maples are shockingly red.

We can't speculate about what's next on our doorstep.

~**Fried Green Tomatoes**

—2 firm green tomatoes
—buttermilk, about a cup
—flour
—salt and pepper
—yellow cornmeal
—peanut oil

Cut tomatoes into 1/2" slices, discarding top and bottom. Make a dredging station with a shallow bowl of buttermilk, one of seasoned flour, and one of cornmeal. Pat tomato slices in flour, dredge in buttermilk and then in cornmeal. Set aside while you do the same for all tomato slices. Heat about an inch of peanut oil in a frying pan on medium heat (cast iron is best). Fry slices on both sides until golden brown and drain on paper towels. Sprinkle with a bit of salt. (Serves 4.)

Omnivore

I have no issue with oysters, sea urchins, okra.
In a sorority initiation, I was force-fed chocolate-covered ants
and imagined them M & M's. Neither aged cheese nor anchovies
drive me from dinner. Bring on frog's legs or sweetbreads a la Jacques
Pépin!

Certain varmints won't be at my barbecue:
nutria on a skewer or squirrel stew like the one
hunters used to make. I'll not forget its claws
peeping out of the gravy, oozy with oil.

If I lived in the Ozarks, didn't have a dime,
I might make different gustatory choices,
might take a pot shot at a ringtail or possum,
slipping off skin like a disposable glove.

Herbivores are better for the planet
and not all vegetables are boring or tame:
wild ramps, blood oranges, dragon fruit,
kohlrabi, and kumquats, for example.

What a smorgasbord is offered every day!
Plucking truffles from rotted logs, steeping pennyroyal
for a carminative tea, cracking a coconut with a machete,
wisely picking and choosing. I want to live to a ripe old age.

~Oyster Bake

—1 pint (or a little more) of fresh shucked oysters
—1 1/2 crumbled saltine crackers or bread crumbs
—1/2 c. melted butter
—2 T. half-and-half or cream
—2 t. melted butter
—salt and pepper

Drain oysters. Mix together saltines or bread crumbs and 1/2 c. melted butter. Cover a pie pan with some of the crumb mixture. Layer with oysters, half-and-half or cream, and 2 t. melted butter. Salt and pepper. Sprinkle top with remaining cracker or bread crumbs. Bake at 400 for 30 minutes. Makes a nice appetizer at Christmas or Christmas Eve dinner. (Serves 6.)

Ode to Okra

The small green pods are
        tender, sweet
                seeping with mucilage
                        carbohydrate-laden, sticky.

Sliced lengthwise, they're cooked down
        with Spanish onions, tomatoes,
                a little corn off the cob,
                        seeds a' pop in your mouth.

Chunked, they thicken
        gumbo and Creole stews
                redolent with andouille,
                      hot peppers, shrimp.

Slender boys with hats
        dance amid the sassafras
                cuddling with oysters
                      American s-m-o-o-o-th!

In cornmeal robes, they snap
        sizzle in hot oil
                one of three by country ham,
                      catfish, chicken legs.

Okra, Abyssinian ancient,
        your weeping tears strengthen,
                emulsify
                      weak broths and bonds.

Oh, that more would plant you,
        admire your winged white flowers,
                or purchase you, sample some,
                      so good for the heart.

~Gumbo

—1 T. flour   —2 diced boneless chicken breasts
—1 T. butter   —2 c. chicken broth

- —1 chopped onion
- —1 chopped green pepper
- —2 chopped celery stalks
- —1/2 T. chopped garlic
- —1 c. sliced andouille or smoked sausage
- —1 14-oz. can diced tomatoes (or chop fresh, skinless tomatoes)
- —1/2 t. dried thyme
- —1 bay leaf
- —1/4 t. cayenne pepper
- —salt and pepper to taste (1/t. filé powder, optional)

In a heavy pot combine flour and butter; cook on medium heat, stirring until roux is light chocolate brown. Add onion, pepper, celery, and garlic; sauté for two minutes. Add the next seven ingredients; simmer on low for 50 minutes. Add salt and pepper to taste and filé powder, if using. Discard bay leaf. Serve over rice. (For extra tasty gumbo, toss in some peeled, deveined shrimp before filé and cook until pink.) (Serves 6)

Mushrooms

I was surprised when my friend told me she did not like mushrooms, though we were in a tavern, and they were served in a basket, deep fried with a garlicky aioli. Perhaps she had encountered a stinkhorn or was afraid of a death cap that resembles a common button mushroom but wreaks havoc with your liver. Maybe it was a bad trip on psilocybin, "shrooms" which induced hallucinations—headless men and winged panthers—when she was really seeking the doors of perception. In a Pima chant a boy ingests peyote and shape-shifts into a dragonfly, then into a rabbit, only to become a man. Mushrooms are fungi so an aversion to spores and mold-like substances is understandable. One doesn't forget, however, delicious concoctions of chanterelles, enokis, portabellas, and creminis, sautés with porcinis or hens-of-the-wood, stir fries chockful of shitakes or morels sautéed with butter and shallots. One summer a Bayport, Minnesota restaurant featured morels in every course, even dessert. A French teacher gave me a bagful gathered in a dying apple orchard. Along with fiddlehead ferns, morels are the jewels of a Mayday meal. Taoist monks believe that mushrooms symbolize peaceful times. They can represent the enchanted, like elves and fairies perched upon mushroom or toadstool tops. Dear Alice sought advice from a hookah-smoking caterpillar upon a mushroom cap. Not everyone can be a mycologist or a lover of mushrooms, but after a rainstorm I appreciate the way they dot the wet grass. I savor them robed in tempura.

Taste

Of the five essential tastes—
salty, sweet, sour, bitter, umami—
bitter is a fascination, often spat out.

Yet it is savored as Starbuck's
dark coffee, cocoa, hops, citrus peel,
tonic, a bed of escarole or chicory
beneath a roasted monkfish.

Bitter herbs at Seder are dipped in salt.

Bitter melon can be stir fried.

A psychic wound can leave a bitter taste
rising in the gut to the mouth.

Some people are bitter.

It's hard to be around them,
their bitterness, long-lived,
never shaking the dirt free,
never getting to the sweet.

Gluttony

Heading out of the Dunkin' drive-thru,
I peek into the magic box of twelve to find
cream-filled Bismarcks, jelly donuts, chocolate-
covered creations, and plain glazed, staring
at me with Cyclopean eyes, bringing to mind
the gluttons in Circle Three who, as on earth,
wallow in waste. Cerberus with slavering fangs
drools over those who loved too much lard-flaked
dough, spits of greasy meat, bread and butter,
and goblets of wine now fatty, vaporous
bodies fouled by offal and slushy rain,
who so loved to smack and lick their lips,
we gluttons who can't pass up a donut shop, an emporium
of fudge. I think of Ciacco swelling like a tick,
Plutus 'round the bend, and take a bite of the blueberry
(because that one is good for you), looking forward
to the day—lunch, dinner, another donut.

A Story of Yams

The African creator Ruwa planted a yam tree, his delight, his nectar. His was no Garden of Eden, fully lush, jungley, proliferate with sunning geckoes, lambs and lions spraddled side-by-side, but a Kilimanjaron paradise overlooking mist and juniper, a mix of forest and barren crags. The tree, heavy with knobby yams, sans devil-entwined twig, lured a wanderer, gender inconsequential, who ate of the yam without any prompting hiss or whispered promises. Ruwa, away on a mission—baboon briefing? green wood hoopoe haranguing?—returned to his world to find the favored plant pilfered. And so, he cursed the human race—*miserere*—who lost immortality all because of the deliciousness of yam. Ruwa rose up onto the mountain peak and looked down on the puny, the powerless, enshrouding the land laced with shadows and those pondering their own, establishing a new world order, selfishness and greed at the heart of the story, power taking precedence once again, all in a man-god's hands which could be perpetually filled with yams if he so desired.

~Sweet Potato/Yam Casserole

—4 pounds sweet potatoes or yams, peeled and cut crosswise into 3/4-inch-thick slices
—1/3 c. packed dark brown sugar
—1/2 t. salt
—1/4 t. coarsely ground black pepper
—4 T. butter (1/2 stick), cut into small pieces
—1/2 c. coarsely chopped walnuts

Preheat oven to 400 degrees. Arrange half of the potato slices in a 13"x 9" ceramic or glass baking dish. Sprinkle with half of the sugar, half of the salt, and all of the pepper. Dot with half of the butter. Arrange the rest of the potatoes in baking dish. Sprinkle with remaining sugar and salt, and dot with remaining butter or margarine. Cover with foil and bake for 30 minutes. Remove foil; sprinkle with walnuts and bake, uncovered for another 30 to 40 minutes longer until potatoes are tender, basting with syrup in baking dish three times during cooking. (Serves 8.)

Taco King, Minnesota State Fair

Maria taps me on the head with an empty box,
"For luck," she says and goes on stuffing
tacos with ground beef, lettuce, cheese,
and a perfect soupcon of diced tomato.
She plays the Gypsy Kings on a cassette player,
hums, and sways, turning to heat refried beans
in the microwave, stirring the mush after the ding.
There's a line down the block, customers staring
at the Texas-born *senoras* building burritos and nachos *grande*,
filling up bottles of fresh salsa loved for its afterburn.
They speak Spanish amongst themselves, and we *gringos*
try a few words like *queso, pollo, and frijoles.*
Their many children come around and hang out
in the back supply tent, sampling tostadas drizzled
with hot liquid cheese and jumbo Mountain Dews.
"I just love this place," a woman wearing pig ears
exclaims. "It's my first stop at the Fair!"
Others want the fresh salsa recipe which the ladies tell them
is easy with a super-duper blender, tomato filets,
white onions, and jalapenos. That's all it is after all.
Oh, and a little salt. At the end of the day, fireworks bursting,
a trickle of drunks orders what's left of the burritos.
Maria pulls out the last tissue to wrap the last taco,
knocks me on the head with the box and says,
"*Por suerte.*" A street cleaner whirrs brushes on the pavement.
A mélange of chicken bits, plastic trays, corn chips,
and lettuce strips go 'round and 'round. All the hard-working
women walk to their cars. Luck has nothing to do with it.

Tomatoes

were once called poison for leaching lead from pewter plates;
thought to be like deadly belladonna, kin of nightshade;
feared for attracting the green hornworm, Argus-eyed pest.
Thomas Jefferson, dispelling fears, ate tomatoes as we did
as children, big bites, freshly picked, explosive juices
dripping down our hands onto our arms,
warmed by the sun in a bristly garden or over
a farmhouse sink with a sprinkle of salt.

Solanum lycopersicum, you are common
like everyday dishes: Big Boys, beefsteak, Early Girl, grape,
or you are heirloom like the wedding china we never use:
Banana Legs, Brandywine, Dutchman, Green Zebra, Hillbilly.
You are famous and beloved: Tiny Tim, Abraham Lincoln,
Paul Robeson. At Central Grocery in New Orleans,
after a muffuletta, I purchased San Marzano seeds which grew
and gave up pulp for a perfect Pomodoro, a garlicky marinara.

Would that all that is poisonous or feared
would turn, like richest alchemy, into wholesomeness,
lusciousness, enrichment! Like tomatoes, we gather
them in rather than push them away like so many things
sown in man-made shadow-splashed plots.

—Tomato Pie

—4 medium garden tomatoes, peeled and sliced
—about 10 fresh basil leaves
—1/2 c. chopped scallion
—1 9-inch prebaked pie shell
—1 c. grated mozzarella
—1 c. grated cheddar, can use a sharp cheddar
—1 c. good mayonnaise, like Duke's
—salt and pepper to taste

Preheat oven to 350. Place tomatoes in colander and sprinkle with salt to drain for about 10 minutes. Dab a little. Layer tomato, basil, and scallion in pie shell. Season with salt and pepper. Combine cheeses and mayo. Spread on top of tomato mixture and bake for 30 minutes. Serve warm. (Serves six.) This is a delicious side dish or light luncheon dish in the summer. The tomatoes must be home grown and ripe for best flavors.

Church Ladies

My husband told me about the Lebanese enclave
on the West Side of St. Paul, shopping at Morgan's
for flat bread and olives, his mother digging up dandelion greens,
pulling grape leaves from a chain link fence.

He remembers Aunts Mary, Janet, Jamila, and Amelia
sipping coffee at the table, gossiping about neighbors,
rolling out bread, five offerings for holy communion,
the mother of God, the angels and saints, the living, the dead.
Mostly, he remembers words: *mishwi, kafta, kusa, baba ghannuj,
hummus bit-tahini, lubyi, falafel, laban, zlaby, shish-ta-aook.*
Every Tuesday was *yakhnit*, chicken stewed in tomatoes and onions
with raw *kibbeh*, sprinkled with pine nuts.

I attempt to re-create what only his mother could create, hanging
yogurt enmeshed in oozing cheesecloth to the kitchen spigot;
breaking vermicelli into sizzling olive oil; coring zucchini to stuff
with rice and lamb; marinating chicken with lemon and garlic;
pureeing baked eggplant with tahini, not as good as what the ladies
made at the Holy Family, a little Lebanese church amid a mélange
of German, Irish, Polish, and Mexican families with foods all their own.

He misses the soft voices with guttural accents, his mother's pickled
turnips and green olives. He remembers the stained-glass window
etched with his father's name, the intonation of Aramaic, St. Maron,
bake sales, bingo in the basement, women serving tabbouleh, beef kebabs,
the smell of billowing incense swung upon a golden chain.

~Shish-ta-aook (Lebanese Chicken)

—1 c. olive oil
—3/4 c. fresh lemon juice
—1 t. ground ginger
—Salt and pepper (about 3/4 teaspoon of each)
—Several smashed cloves of garlic (I use about four but use to taste)

Mix all ingredients together to make marinade. Marinate about 8 to 10 pieces of white chicken meat (boned or boneless) and/or chicken thighs overnight in the marinade. The next day, remove from marinade and grill or broil. If using pieces, you may skewer as with shish-ka-bob. Serve with rice, pita bread, and garlic or tahini sauce. (Serves 8.)

On the Way to the Post Office

A web of branches before me,
        hoarfrost on the trees,
                the errand, vaporizes.

As in spring, purple hyacinth
        pocking the crystalline labyrinth
                beneath a lollipop tree.

As in summer, myriad marvels:
        foxglove, yarrow, peony,
                dahlias, delphinium-diving bees.

As in fall, brilliant sumac,
        cherried bric-a-brac
                dotting a hillside.

Loss and thoughts of loss, eased,
        amid corollas, arcs, and light
                illuminating dark spaces.

Distractions from disasters, notifications
        of disease, stuff of daily news,
                lifting in the wink of sun.

It isn't then about a roll of stamps,
        meat at the market, or lack of parking,
                the sublime in stillness all around.

End of November 2020

Near a trifurcated trunk at pond's edge
in a sliver of open water,
a gulping mouth arose
to consume something
still alive, sere oak leaves afloat.

A good sign, this,
with over 100 deaths
in a single day for our state
in a country silent
except wind in pine.

A walk by the Mississippi yesterday,
a lone bald eagle circled
the noiseless woods.

Is this surrender?

Inside, the work of pie,
cutting shortening into flour,
crimping edges, dollops of cream.

Outside, what is meant to be.

Prayer can happen without thought,
hammer of heart, wistful looking,
grace, hunger exalted.

Letting Go

Autumn is here. I must escape to the mountains.
I am masked and gloved and flying.

I have a nephew in prison,
let's call him Lee. His mother
will be 80 the day he's out.

A nun once told me, "Lost time is never found."

Lee plays the drums like Lars Ulrich
but with COVID he lost music room
privileges. He eats baloney sandwiches in his cell.

The staff refused a hardback book
about Metallica I sent him.
Soft covers only.

When there's fog, prisoners are locked down.

Two rivers flow nearby.
An abattoir of shrikes, a bouquet of warblers
shrouds over a southern battlefield.

A little boy collects rust and reddish leaves.
He pastes them in a book where the glue
will harden, the leaves, crack.

I walk in the pied woods by the Big House range.

A blue moon is rising soon.

Whither

Map on an autumn leaf,
GPS of wind, whispering
Siri in snowfall, guide me.

What aimless walks I have taken,
stuck but now unstuck
as choices made in a yellow wood!

Too, I have floundered in uncharted
waters, unable to touch,
a gulp of undoing lake.

Foam-flogged shores,
trampled wheat, storm-blown ibis—
you speak, tell truths, lead

as counselors of earth,
advisors of air,
witnesses of water.

You were there all along,
a recommendation of rhododendron,
a parental hand of river branch.

Directions
> *The man pulling radishes pointed my way with a radish.*
> —*Kobayashi Issa*

It likely started when I got lost
in the Hampton Roads Bridge Tunnel
on my way to see *Waiting for Godot,*
traversing the claustrophobic conduit,
picturing water and walls pressing in.
I'm directionally challenged, being left-
brained, lacking some of that spatial
and mathematical functioning needed
to navigate this world. I have been known
to hold a map upside-down, misread images
in mirrors or cameras when trying
to coordinate a move. The biggest
arguments between me and my significant
other always have to do with directions.
I, telling him to stop at the nearest gas
station, unashamed to ask for a landmark,
a turn, a distance. Please do not thrust
a cell phone in my hand and tell me
to track the pulsating arrow
or pinch the screen in and out to find
roads like arteries winding around and around.
A friendly uninflected GPS voice
or Siri on a cell now tells us
when to turn right or left.
I still have to have some idea
of the destination since the robotic lady
once drove me right to the lip
of White Bear Lake. Ironically, I love
to go, to drive, to travel. If only I had
the instincts of a Bedouin, the confidence
of a scout or New York taxi driver but even
the most confident Uber relies on tech,
and more importantly, right-brain savvy,
a pinging in the head leading safely home.

Is this the zombie apocalypse everyone talks about?

People walking past each other, snake eyes looking neither right
nor left, ear buds occluding ears, mesmerized
by phones glued to hands, flesh and blood people
right there, right next to them, say, on a bus bench
or at a concert. Twice today I had to say "excuse me"
to two different women in Hy-Vee, one yacking on the phone
while perusing dried mac and cheese, one texting
furiously before Asian condiments, canned chow mein.
They sluggishly stepped aside, eyes never meeting mine,
no "Oh, sorry" or "Hi, didn't see you there."
Shopping over, I joined the slowest line, glanced at by a harried cashier
who, at the end of the transaction, mindlessly dangled
a receipt, picked up her cell and began chatting.
Two days later in the airport I am the only one at the gate
not staring at a phone or laptop while we wait to board
the late plane. People are nice enough as they shuffle
along with overstuffed carry-ons, jamming them into overhead
bins, bumping legs on the way to window seats, jostling
the already-seated playing Candy Crush or solitaire on I-pads.
After turbulence and tiredness overwhelm us,
we sleep, awaking in a different state, staring at seatbacks,
fumbling for cell phones warming our gonads,
telling our loved ones, "We are here." For a moment,
we are human again, bursting out of exits, rushing to hug,
to kiss, loading up the car, riding out into the dark.

~Chicken Chow Mein Casserole

—1 3-ounce package of chow mein noodles
—1 can cream of mushroom soup
—1/4 c. water
—1 can water chestnuts, sliced
—1/2 c. slightly chopped cashews
—1/4 c. chopped onions
—1 c. celery, diced
—1 c. green peppers, diced
—2 cups cooked chicken, cubed

Mix all but 1/2 cup of chow mein noodles. Pour mixture into 1-1/2-quart casserole and top with remaining noodles. Bake for 40 minutes at 325 degrees. Serve with soy sauce if desired. (Serves 4.)

A Spring Trip after Russia Declares War

Down by Biloxi's shore, a country boy who told us he loved
chicken gizzards and turnip greens drove a cab that smelled of seafood
near a white spit of beach, a shoal of porpoises on the hunt,
a sea hawk overhead, scars of Katrina along Highway 90.

This haven from winter warmed the bones, the casino offering
bad tuna melts and Gulf breezes. A loud woman poked a slot machine.
No one questioned the lack of service since the pandemic,
tolerating soiled linen, wet carpet, a busy signal to the front desk.

My husband played poker and won a hand, bluffing with a pair of nines.
I bought a pie bird, Polish pottery, thinking about the Poles
who provided baby buggies and homes for fleeing Ukrainians
the least I could do on a free four-day spree.

Above the veranda, a Coast Guard copter buzzed, keeping watch.
A homeless man on a pier ate from a bin while we breakfasted
on cathead biscuits, shrimp and grits. I never found a newspaper,
seeking news about the war, climate change. A storm blew in.

On the last day, we watched our luggage hauled to the airport,
rain pelting the tour bus, donning masks for the flight home.
Somewhere in the distance, a siren sounded, a tornado warning.
Somewhere in Kyiv, people huddled in bomb shelters, lit candles.

~Shrimp and Grits

—2 c. water
—1 14-oz. can low salt chicken broth
—1/4 c. half-and-half
—1 c. regular grits
—3/4 c. shredded cheddar cheese
—1/4 c. grated Parmesan
—2 T. butter
—1/2 t. Tabasco sauce
—1/4 t. white pepper
—3 slices bacon

—1 lb. peeled and deveined shrimp, dusted in flour
—1/4 t. black pepper
—1/8 t. salt
—1 c. sliced button mushrooms
—1/2 c. chopped scallions
—2 minced garlic cloves
—1/2 c. low sodium chicken broth
—2 T. fresh lemon juice
—1/4 t. Tabasco sauce
—lemon wedges, chopped tomatoes

Bring first 4 ingredients to a boil in a med. pan; slowly whisk in grits. Lower heat and simmer, stirring occasionally, 10 min. or until thick. Add cheeses, butter, Tabasco and white pepper. Keep warm. Cook bacon in skillet until crisp; drain on paper towels and keep 1 T. drippings in pan (may also add a little butter). Crumble bacon and set aside. Sprinkle shrimp with salt and pepper. Sauté mushrooms in drippings/butter until soft. Add scallions and sauté 2 minutes. Add shrimp and cook. Stir in broth, lemon juice, and Tabasco. Cook 2 min. Stir to loosen "goodies" from pan. Serve shrimp with crumbled bacon, sliced lemon wedges, and a sprinkling of fresh chopped tomatoes. (serves 4)

The Cheese Stands Alone
"Poets have been mysteriously silent on the subject of cheese."
~Gilbert K. Chesterton

They themselves speak of meadows, cool winds,
Jerseys, guernseys, Swiss, shorthorns, reds,
chewing cuds and grasses, or bleating goats,
Nigerian dwarfs, Boers, Alpines.

They themselves speak of places:
County Cork, Parma, Mykonos,
Oaxaca, Gouda, Leicester,
Roquefort, Sheboygan, Philly.

Blame the silence on a mouthful
of cheddar, the melt on pies
tomato or otherwise, tuna surprise,
a muttering of mozzarella.

Blame the silence on war,
suffering, injustice.
Things that need our verses,
voices in the wilderness.

I want to break the silence
as after a blessing at table,
passing and sharing plates, stories,
eyes meeting over cheese and fruit.

I want to hand a hunk of cheese, a slice of bread
to a hungry refugee, a freedom lover
who simply wants to be home,
making *hrudka*, kettle singing.

Task at Hand
> "No, I do not weep at the world—I am too busy sharpening my oyster knife".
> ~Zora Neale Hurston

The stars slide into rest.
Go ahead and forget.

You gaze out the kitchen window,
a soapy dish in your hand.

Your face reflects in the cold pane.

A busy squirrel cleans his face like a fly
and flattens, absorbing final heat.

The world is somewhere out there.
The work of our hands—mighty rubble.

Leave the world behind, unwept for,
the last plate unwashed.

A cloud of suds winks in the sink
in the snap of new darkness.

May Day

I turn south when spring comes north,
opening up, a transplanted bay oyster,
to the rhythms of original tide, envisioning wrap
of blue mountains, dogwood buds, azalea
in bloom—here, ice clings to water,
snow weaves woods.
I am a rose-breasted grosbeak,
a Blackburnian warbler, winging
back, singing sky. I am an early ephemeral,
bluebell or bloodroot, deep like the corm,
nourished, re-emerging.
Something like phototropism stirs me,
moves me until I don't.

Notes

- *Callinectes sapidus*, the scientific name for blue crab, translates to "savory beautiful swimmers."
- Haystacks Calhoun: a Texas-born heavyweight pro wrestler
- The Cowardly Lion's words about courage are adapted from E. Y. Harburg's lyrics to "If I Were King of the Forest."
- *Hagstrom* in Swedish translates to "cherry tree dweller by a stream." The B52's wrote the song "Rock Lobster" and "Love Shack" ("tin roof, rusted"); R.E.M. wrote the song "It's the End of the World as We Know It (I Feel Fine)." The Northrop and Lind Hall are on the University of MN campus, Minneapolis.
- " O O O O that Shakespeherian Rag!" is from "The Waste Land" by T.S. Eliot; "Wheel in the sky keeps on turning" is from the song "Wheel in the Sky" by Journey.
- 100 deaths refer to one Minnesota daily death count during the COVID pandemic, November 2020
- *Hrudka* is a Ukrainian soft cheese made around Easter time.
- Marine biologists tell of Chesapeake Bay oyster beds transplanted into Lake Michigan that still open and shut to the original tidal rhythms of the bay.

Acknowledgments

Thank you to the original publishers of these works or forms thereof:
- "In the Tilling": *North/South Blogspot*, 2019.
- "The Tiptons": *Rewilding Hope,* (LOMP Press), 2023.
- "Artichokes": *The Penn Review*, 2019.
- "Berry is My Madeleine": *AvantAppal(achia)*, Issue 7, 2019.
- "Picking Asparagus": *Poetry Virginia*, 2021.
- "Where the River Ran": *North/South Blogspot,* 2019.
- "Mist," *Earth's Daughters: Illusions*, 2023.
- "Apricots": *ArLiJo*, Issue 158, Gival Press, 2022.
- "Off": *Sleet*, 2012.
- "Distant Lightning,": *Agates*, 2022.
- "Circle Dance," *Sandcutters*, 2020.
- "On Blindness: *Genre: Urban Arts*, #8, 2019.
- "Teeth": *Genre: Urban Arts,* #8, 2019.
- "Till Death Do Us Part": *Typishly,* 2018.
- "Early October, 2020": *This Was* 2020, Ramsey Co. Library, 2021.
- "Tomatoes": *Crosswinds Poetry Journal*, Volume II, 2017.
- "Church Ladies": *The Saint Paul Almanac*, Volume 12, 2019.
- "End of November": *Sunday Morning Lyricality*, 2021.
- "Whither": *Conestoga Zen*, 2021.
- "Is this the zombie apocalypse everyone talks about?": *Whistling Shade*, May 2020.
- "The Cheese Stands. Alone," Dakota Co. Library website, 2022.
- "Task at Hand," *Freshwater Review*, 2022.

Recipes: Courtesy of Janice Bageant, "Bernie" Francis Pleasants, Kathleen Zajac, Dolores Trojan, Anne Marie Rierdon, Anne Godson, Barbara Weiss, Viola Higgs Pleasants, Kathleen Aronson, Patricia Swenson, Mary Lou Pleasants Grundtner, Tina Isaac, Janice Belden, and the author.

After earning English degrees from James Madison University, Virginia, and the University of Minnesota, **Donna Isaac** received her MFA from Hamline University in 2007 where she was awarded Best Poetry Thesis for her capstone, *Sustenance*. She taught English and writing in the Shenandoah Valley of Virginia and in the Twin Cities, Minnesota, retiring from full-time work after 40 years. She continues to work with community poetry through the League of MN Poets. Published work includes chapbooks: *Tommy* (Red Dragonfly Press); *Holy Comforter* (Red Bird Chapbooks); and *Persistence of Vision* (Finishing Line Press) and a poetry book, *Footfalls* (Pocahontas Press). Her writing appears in various journals including the *Penn Review, The Saint Paul Almanac*, and others. <donnaisaacpoet.com>

www.ingramcontent.com/pod-product-compliance
Lightning Source LLC
Chambersburg PA
CBHW030055170426
43197CB00010B/1528